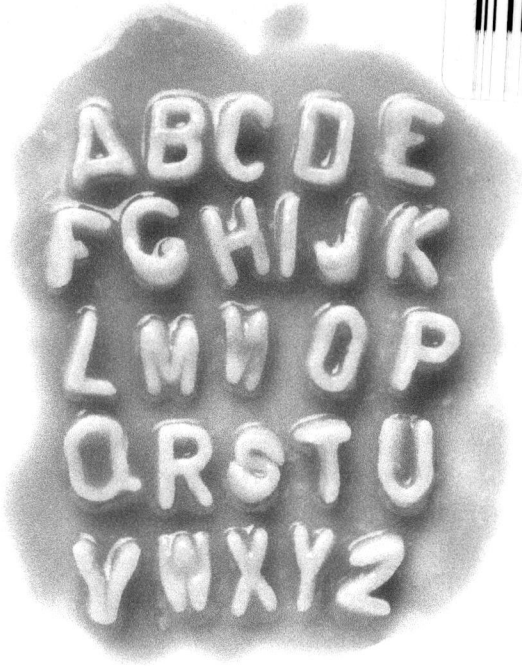

THE POCKET GUIDE
TO MARKETING SPEAK
Stop Mouthing the Words and Start Using Them

....

Michelle Kabele

IDEASTORM PRESS

ISBN: 978-0-9820686-4-9
Library of Congress Control Number: 2008938656

INTRODUCTION

"We can't launch the site until IT looks at the metrics from the beta."

"Be sure to grab the CTR and CPC so we can begin to calculate ROI from the WOM campaign."

"In the meantime, run a SWOT, and let's test the line's elasticity."

"Are we thinking of differentiation between channels?"

How fluent is your Marketing Speak? Are you following this exchange? The language of the marketing world continues to evolve. The Internet introduced new opportunities for marketers, expanded channels, and basically gave a new look to this already complex business need. If you're struggling to "talk the talk", believe me, you're not alone! I've compiled this dictionary to give you definitions of the terms you're encountering and to offer some insight as to how you can (and probably *should*) be integrating them into your daily marketing efforts.

To make this book user-friendly, The Pocket Guide to Marketing Speak:

Stop Mouthing the Words and Start Using Them lists the terms alphabetically. At the end of the guide, I've included a special section that groups terms by category. So, if you need to focus your conversation on email marketing or marketing mix you can peruse the list of topics and look up the other words you probably should know.

Following these entries, I've included a list of acronyms, everything from "AOL" to "WWW". Sure, these are the easier terms, but do you also know what "CPC," "PFP," and "UGC" stand for?

Keep a copy of The Pocket Guide to Marketing Speak: Stop Mouthing the Words and Start Using Them in your desk drawer, your laptop case, and on top of that stack of magazines and reports you need to read. And, unlike your average dictionary, take the time to read this book from the first entry to the last because you'll gain more than a definition. You'll get facts and a slew of mini-lessons that could make you rethink the way you conduct your marketing.

ACTION PLAN. In order to tackle a set of tasks in a timely, efficient manner, you need to develop an action plan that identifies the specific tasks, the person(s) responsible for each task, and a timeline. The tasks within an action plan should be measurable and designed to meet a specific objective, such as implementing marketing promotion, creating an e-commerce site, increasing sales over a specified period, etc.

ADVERTISER. The term refers to the manufacturer, owner, or provider of a product or service who pays to advertise that product or service using any of a vast array of media (e.g. newspaper, magazine, billboard, transit, pay-per-click, banner, television, radio).

ADVERTISING. The component within the marketing mix that directly communicates a selling message, paid for and delivered through a specific medium, such as print, broadcast (commercials), online, and outdoor (e.g., billboards). A typical ad delivers a single message to a large number of people (e.g., reach, circulation, audience, viewers, visitors) — a mass, non-personal promotion that still has its place in this highly personalized, customized marketing arena.

This mass-approach has always been potentially inefficient for a couple of reasons. First, any given message most likely exceeds its target market, meaning that advertising dollars are spent both on people who will respond to the message…and many who won't. Second, advertising has a track-record of being a one-way form of marketing, with the message being sent directly to the receiver. Thankfully the winds of change are headed this way. A growing number of advertising technologies and media outlets are offering more personalized and targeted messages, particularly through online vehicles. Technological advances will allow television viewers, for instance, to simply click a button for more information on the given product or service and eventually be able to access/order that product right then and there with an Internet connection.

ADSENSE. Google provides a way for website owners to make some extra money on their sites by featuring Google ads from their AdWords pay-per-click system. Launched in 2003, AdSense ads are produced by Google with JavaScript and generate revenue on a per-click or per-impression basis. Advertisements are customized to site content, the user's geographical location, etc. AdSense's growing popularity comes from ads that are less intrusive than banners and with content that is relevant to the given website.

AdSense has proven successful in helping websites monetize their content, a particularly appealing bonus for small websites that lack sufficient resources for sales programs and staff. But before you expect big revenue from AdSense advertisements, be aware that the bigger money-makers are on sites that not only get heavy traffic but that post keywords that earn high bids from the pay-per-click advertisers. Think about it: If an advertiser is forced to pay $2 per click, you stand to make more money here than from an advertiser who has won the keyword bid at 25 cents per click!

ADWORDS (AKA GOOGLE ADWORDS). Launched in 2000, AdWords is Google's flagship advertising product and multi-billion dollar revenue source. Based on pay-per-click and site-targeted advertising for both text and banner ads, the program offers local, national, and international placement on websites. Ads are always short — like mini-billboards or classified ads — and advertisers specify the key words that trigger their ads and state the maximum amount they are willing to pay per click. Their sponsored links show up, cued by key words typed into the search engine.

Google places the paid listings depending on the advertisers PPC and the quality score of all ads for any given search. They also set the minimum bids for an advertiser's keywords. The formula for determining these things is a cryptic and dynamic formula for Google, but one that marketers don't balk at as they keep coming back for more.

AFFILIATE. While not truly a middle-man, the affiliate does the dance thatbrings both merchant and purchaser to the party. The affiliate gives wider distribution to the merchant's products in return for performance-based compensation (i.e., commission). The distribution source is usually website traffic or email list subscribers. The affiliate owns and/or operates the website that drives traffic to the other site.

Using Internet marketing tools such as search engine optimization, search engine marketing, email marketing and displays, affiliates create seam-less, user-friendly relationships between their clients and the customers.

AFFILIATE MARKETING. Simply put, this kind of marketing uses one website to drive traffic to another, non-competitor site. The end result is revenue sharing between online advertisers/merchants and online publishers/salespeople. The performance-based compensation is based on sales, clicks, registrations, or some hybrid model. Amazon's ever-expanding offerings represent a powerful affiliate marketing program.

What are the benefits of this simple arrangement? There are lots of them, including automation of much of the marketing process (accepting and approving applications, generating unique links, tracking and reporting results) and payment only for tangible results (actual sales, registrants, clicks, etc.). Advertising and marketing is inherently risky, and this model shifts most of the responsibility from merchants to affiliates.

ALGORITHM. A term you're likely to hear about in any discussion of search engines, algorithms drive computer programs with sequences of instructions that tell the computer how to solve a particular problem. Written in a language that a computer can understand, an algorithm must be specified exactly and must have a finite number of steps. In general terms, an algorithm can also be a set of steps for a person to follow. Search engines have algorithms that determine their method for evaluating a site and establishing page ranking. In the early days of the search engines, it didn't take long for hackers to figure out these algorithms and find ways to "beat the system" and boost sites to top rankings. As a result, the search engines' algorithms are changed regularly, and they vary from one engine to another.

ANALYTICS. A common buzzword in the online world, analytics refers to the statistical data compiled for a specific function process, such as click-through, buying habits, and transactional data.

ARTICLE DIRECTORY (AKA ARTICLE BANK). If an e-zine merged with an encyclopedia, the offspring would likely be an article directory. This online source gathers articles posted online and organizes them by topic. The content is usually free to the visitor, while the articles' authors pay a small fee to submit the articles. An ideal source for research, article directories like ezine.com, isnare.com, ideamarkteters.com, and articledashboard.com present a seemingly limitless volume of invaluable research, opinions, and insight from thought leaders in every conceivable industry and subject area.

ARTICLE MARKETING. The Internet has become the research tool of choice for anyone with access, thus making it a desirable resource for marketing. While professionals have long been publishing articles in the media to promote their knowledge, the use of the Internet for a similar purpose creates an unlimited reach. Thought leaders (and wanna-be's) use article marketing to submit their works to article directories, which feed to other directories. The viral effect spreads the articles, which can be picked up with organic searches.

AUTO-RESPONDER. This computer program (also known as an infobot, mailbot, automailer, or email responder) automatically answers emails sent to it. The first auto-responders were created within mail transfer agents when they couldn't reach a particular address. We've all seen these "your email could not be delivered…" type messages. Since then, auto-responders have evolved as email marketing tools. They are frequently used to confirm subscriptions, purchases, payments, posts, inquiries, and other such things. They deliver information to customers and follow up with them at preset times. There are two types:

• Outsourced ASP models operate on the provider's system, making them easy to implement for the end-user. You pay a monthly usage fee. TrafficWave.net, GetResponse, and Aweber offer these hosted auto-responder services.

- Server-side models enable users to install an auto-responder system on their own server. This is much more technical, but if you've got the staff for it, it's also cost-effective. Check out AutoResponsePlus and ListMailPro.

BANNER AD. These online ads typically feature a prominent headline or title extending across the full-page width of the ad space. Like billboard ads along the roadways, banner ads are designed to grab your attention, driving you to click through to the site for more about the latest program or affiliate.

BLOG. Short for "weblog", a blog is a website that features an online journal of thoughts, musings, opinions, ideas, and, yes, even product knowledge. Some of the millions of blog sites on the Internet are more informational and include lists of resources on the Web while others are purely for chatting. An open blog welcomes the input from other readers while a closed blog delivers a one-way discussion from the host blogger. Blogs have soared in popularity with the rise of social networking; as a result, many businesses have joined the crowd. A blog is easy to start with the help of free hosting services such as WordPress and Blogger.

BLOGGER. He or she who blogs; also the name of one of the top blog hosting services.

BLOGOSPHERE. The interconnected universe of blogs and bloggers is known as the "blogosphere".

BOOKMARK. Logically, with millions of pages on the World Wide Web, you need a place holder to get you back to the content you use most often. A bookmark is a link that you save on your Internet browser; also known as "Favorites" on Internet Explorer.

BOT. Short for "robot" (because we love our shortcuts, abbreviations, and acronyms), a bot is a software application that performs automated tasks faster than a human being. Search engine spiders and crawlers are examples of bots, digging through millions of web pages to index the sites.

BRAND/BRAND IDENTITY. A product, service, or company is identified by a name, logo, tagline, and graphic imagery, like the ubiquitous Coca-Cola script, the bold FedEx lettering, and the Apple symbol. More than just a catchy name or symbol, a brand reflects the qualities of the product, service, or company it represents. The crafting of the brand now calculates the mission of the company, the relationship with the customers, and the value proposition that distinguishes it from the competition.

Branding has existed as long as marketing but has become the big buzzword in today's business world where brand reaches deeply into core values and operational efficiencies.

BRAND LOYALTY. The degree to which a consumer continues to purchase a particular brand reflects the brand loyalty. From buying the same deodorant to driving the same brand of car, loyalty is a reflection of that company's success in meeting the needs of the consumer. Studies show that older generations (e.g., Silent Generation and Baby Boomers) are more loyal to brands than members of Gen X and Y, which has redefined branding strategies to companies that cater to this dominant segment. Price shoppers (bargain hunters) are on the bottom of the loyalty ladder since they are easily swayed by cost, not inherent product or service values. With the massive expansion of e-commerce, maintaining brand loyalty amidst an ocean of anonymous competition has become a Herculean task, causing branders to delve into their creative caches to institute loyalty and rewards programs. As a result, consumers have responded in a Pavlovian manner, expecting to be courted with promises of paybacks, "free" gifts, and bonuses.

BREAK-EVEN ANALYSIS. The point at which the net cost of producing (e.g., cost of goods, manufacturing, overhead) and delivering (e.g., transportation, advertising, distribution) a product or service is in balance with the revenue it generates is the break-even point. The break-even analysis considers the fixed costs, variable costs, unit price, and projected sales. This data is used to calculate the route to reaching the break-even point, giving the marketing and sales staff an initial goal.

BROWSER. This software application is your portal into the Internet, helping you to search the vast information highway for whatever you're seeking. The WorldWideWeb was the first browser, launched in 1990, but its name was changed to Nexus to avoid being confused with the much larger World Wide Web. Some of the most common browsers include Netscape, Internet Explorer, Firefox, Mozilla, and Safari.

BUSINESS PLAN. You wouldn't build a house without a blueprint, so why even think of starting or running a business without a business plan? Considered your blueprint for success, a business plan outlines the type of business you plan to operate, who is involved, how it will operate (and by whom), the market segments to be served, a marketing plan, and the financial support that will get it (and keep it) running. Business plans are required when seeking loans or investors, but such a plan is also the best route to maintaining your vision and keeping your company on track.

BUZZ. Whether the conversation occurs around the water cooler or in the vast world of the Internet, "buzz" is the top stories, topics, people, products, and other items that people are talking about. A great place to see what's buzzing on the 'Net is buzz.yahoo.com.

BUZZ MARKETING. Also known as "word-of-mouth marketing", the approach relies on the viral spread of positive messaging from consumer to consumer. Texting, blogging, and social networking have enabled online marketers to harness the power of the Internet to do their bidding.

CALL TO ACTION. For every action, there is a reaction. It's a simple law of physics — and of marketing. The call to action (CTA) is the response the advertiser wants the viewer/reader to take. "Order now", "call today", "click here", and "reserve yours now" are examples of calls to action.

With the exception of image advertising, no promotional bid should ever be without the call to action. Consider yourself the shepherd minding your flock and guiding them to the appropriate gate. A consumer does not necessarily take action without guidance, suggestion, or outright demand!

CAMPAIGN. Just as a presidential campaign spans a promotional effort over months and years, a marketing campaign represents an ongoing program to communicate a message and prompt the desired response among a targeted segment. A campaign can consist of a series of advertisements placed in one or more media over a specified period of time or it can be comprised of an array of promotional elements, such as direct mail, email, advertising, and publicity. To be successful, a campaign should be directed at achieving a measureable, pre-determined result, such as boosting sales, driving traffic to a store or website, increasing market share, or gaining media coverage. Without a scale on which to measure the results of a campaign against the cost expended to implement it, no campaign can ever be a complete success.

CAN-SPAM. The CAN-SPAM Act of 2003 was established to crack down on unwanted emails. The legislation, which falls under the auspices of the Federal Trade Commission, was designed to require marketers to obtain permission from consumers. Like the "Do Not Call" list that has whittled names for telemarketers, the law also requires email marketers to provide in every email a means for the recipient to unsubscribe or "opt out" from an email list. The Controlling the Assault of Non-Solicited Pornography and Marketing Act, like many legislative enforcement acts, reduced spam among the law-abiding people who conformed to permission-based emails. Spammers continue to hit the email boxes in massive volume.

CANNIBALIZATION. There was a time when a company only worried about competition from other businesses. With the advent of multi-channel marketing — involving various sales channels such as catalog, Internet, and brick-and-mortar retail stores — many businesses are seeing their customers shift from making their purchase with another channel within the same corporation. While this cannibalization has no negative impact on the corporate bottom line, individual channels fear for their existence as shoppers opt for their preferred channel. However, top marketing minds have shown that consumers who shop across more than one channel spend considerably more money with the company, making a positive impact on the bottom line. The task remains for the multi-channel marketers to gain the support of individual channels that fear the cannibalization is eating away at their revenue.

CHANNEL. Whether the channel is used for sales or marketing, the term refers to the path taken to get a marketing message, product, or service from the source to the desired recipient. A marketing channel can be print or broadcast advertising, mobile advertising, public relations, direct mail, or any of the online opportunities. A sales channel consists of the various routes to the consumer, including distributor, wholesaler, reseller, retailer, etc., as well as the consumers themselves.

CHANNEL DISTRIBUTION. This system is an organized network of agencies and institutions that perform everything necessary to link producers with end- customers in their marketing feats. The main concern here is the front-end/ distribution channels that move the products/services from company to customer.

In any given channel, some basic steps must be taken to bring the greatest chance for success, regardless of what it is you're marketing.

- Ordering
- Handling and shipping
- Storage
- Display
- Promotion
- Selling
- Information feedback

Regardless of how many players are active in your channel, your products will likely move through several tiers (manufacturers, distributors, dealers), and the above tasks come in to play in one way or another. Making sure that they are handled at appropriate points in the channel gives the greatest chance for creating happy (and repeat) customers.

CHANNEL MARKETING. This marketing style takes an active, customized approach, transforming a sales channel into an effective marketing tool. Combining marketing communications, product marketing and buying incentives, a team creates a direct path for getting its product into the market...and into the hands that want it!

To best use this method, you must constantly identify new channels through which to sell and support your products and services. To maximize your success with channel marketing, find well-positioned and connected partners and train third parties to manage resources. The quintessential channel marketer expertly wields strategic solutions, program and project management, customer communications, database marketing, customer value modeling, partnership marketing, digital marketing, CRM systems, customer service operations, marketing technologies, mailing production and distribution...all customized at every step of the way.

CHANNEL PROMOTION. The "push-pull" methodology of a channel promotion utilizes a combination of incentives to draw interest from both the vendor (retailer, distributor) and end-user. The "push" drives the vendor to purchase the product from the manufacturer and motivates the vendor to actively sell that product to the consumer; examples are spiffs, co-op advertising, buy-get, bundling, and rebates. The "pull" is the promotion that attracts the consumer (end-user), such as a coupon, rebate, buy-get, or bundle.

CHURN RATE. This marketing metric refers to the rate at which customers are defecting from your ranks and taking their business elsewhere. Churn rate is a valuable metric when a company is undergoing change (in products, service levels, pricing) or facing new or stronger competition. When referring to employee exodus, the churn rate is referred to as "turnover"

CIRCULATION. The circulation refers to the actual number of copies of a publication (newspaper, magazine) that is printed and distributed. This is not to be confused with readership, which is an estimation of the number of readers, based on the total number of copies produced and multiplied by a factor known as "pass-along value", which is the number of readers believed to see an individual copy. Those that congregate in the waiting rooms of doctors' offices, for example, will have a higher pass-along value. While this number is usually based on audited surveys, the best means for evaluating the value of a an advertising vehicle is the solid, fact-based numbers, which is paid circulation (not the freebies, because giveaways have no vested interest from the recipient).

CLICK-THROUGH. Click on a link and pass on to another site. In email campaigns, the first measurement a marketer looks at is how many recipients open the email. The second and more important factor measures how many of those recipients clicked on one or more links in the email, because this demonstrates a higher level of interest.

CLICK-THROUGH RATE. The click-through rate (CTR) gauges the success of online and email advertising. The CTR is the percentage of the total clicks from an email or website to get to another page. This is not the same as unique visitors, because one visitor can account for numerous clicks. CTR is an effective tool in identifying the pages on your site that people are visiting most frequently (and those that are being ignored!). It is also a valuable test of emails to determine the messages that trigger more click-throughs. Personalized messages, quirky or unusual formats, or more bold and obtrusive ads tend to have a higher CTR. In a world where more and more business is done in a virtual environment, measures like CTR are essential to the online marketer.

CLIENT. The words "customer" and "client" are often used synonymously, but a client, by definition, results from a relationship, rather than a single transaction. A customer can make a purchase and leave — possibly forever, depending on the buying experience. A client is a buyer in whom you invest time and effort to maintain a relationship. With this definition, Customer Relationship Management should more accurately be *Client* Relationship Management.

CO-OP ADVERTISING. Like the idea of splitting advertising costs with someone else? Co-op (short for "cooperative") provides a means for participating in an ad campaign where the placement costs are supplemented by the manufacturer or other vendor, in order to encourage the wholesaler/distributor/reseller/retailer to promote its products. The amount of co-op dollars available varies, and is usually dependent on the dollar volume of purchases made from the manufacturer. Since all parties have a vested interest in increasing sales, it's a win-win situation.

COOKIE. A cookie is a message that passes from a Web server to your browser, identifying users and text strings like login information. The cookies are then stored on your hard drive (sort of like a cookie jar) because your server maintains no memory. Cookies automatically fill in your online forms. Some sites store your information (customer information, billing, shipping, credit card) which is then encrypted for security purposes. Periodically, you should check the cookies stored in your browser and delete the undesired ones.

Cost Per Conversion represents the cost of acquiring a new customer, an important factor when determining your methods for developing new business. The CPC (not to be confused with Cost Per Click) is determined by dividing the total cost of an ad campaign by the number of actual conversions (a lead, sale, or purchase).

CUSTOMER. A customer is an individual or business without whom you would have no business! They are the purchasers, either as a distributor, wholesaler, retailer, or end-user. And, quite often, your customer is also a sales rep for your company, spreading positive word-of-mouth referrals to prospective buyers. You need customers and you must create the basis for them needing you. Customers are people or organizations that will benefit from the products and/or services offered by your organization. They fall into three general groups:

- *Existing customers* have already purchased or used your products or services, usually within a given-time period. Approximately 80% of your business probably comes from them. It's significantly less expensive and less time-consuming to maintain relationships with existing customers than to create new ones, although that's vital, too.

- *Former customers* are those with whom you've done business but have not maintained an active buy-sell relationship. They either haven't required your products or services for a given time or they have taken their business elsewhere. Their value to you depends on whether or not the business relationship ended (or hopefully paused) on a positive note. If positive, leverage the past relationship to rebuild it, which is still less expensive than cultivating a cold lead.

- *Potential customers* have "Existing Customer" written all over them. They need what you're offering (but probably don't know it yet) and have the means and authority to buy from you! In other words, never rest too easy on past success. Potential customers are the key to growth.

CUSTOMER RELATIONSHIP MANAGEMENT. CRM applies to the process used by a company to handle contact with its customers. With a vast array of software programs to choose from, CRM is a hands-on, user-friendly system to manage information to better serve your customers. The system can be accessed and entered by employees in different departments of a given company and holds details on customer contacts themselves and on any interaction. The sum of the information is used to improve services and fine-tune targeted marketing and sales. CRMs aim to unify and track customer interaction. By organizing information about front and back office operations, business relationships, and analyzing all information for marketing campaigns and strategies, you can better serve your customers AND the future of your company.

DATABASE MARKETING. We all know that Big Brother is watching. Our purchasing habits are no secret to anyone who has access to the right databases, which is any savvy marketer. Using this information, a business can target you with personalized communication — usually via direct mail or email — to send you marketing messages that should appeal to your interests. The non-spam database marketers have your consent to send these messages because you accepted an offer, signed up to receive updates, or otherwise willingly provided your information. Personalized communication has proven to draw a higher response and closure rate than general direct and email campaigns so marketers rely heavily on the quality of their databases and the statistical software used to segment it.

DEFENSIVE MARKETING. This form of marketing focuses on reducing customer dissatisfaction. The defensive approach should be a short-term solution while building a growth strategy because "damage control" offers no potential for increasing market share, but rather presents a last-ditch effort for maintaining existing clients through a rough period. Relationship marketing presents a stronger methodology for both minimizing customer defection and building a larger, more loyal customer base.

DEMOGRAPHICS. If you want to be effective at marketing to a specific audience or segment, you've got to know as much as possible about those prospects. Demographics is the study of the characteristics of group of people — a gathering of quantitative data, such as age, gender, education level, marital status, geographic location, home ownership, household size, income, interests, etc. This information is easy to gather from government/ census data, news media, trade associations, and financial reporting services. A smart marketer also gathers such data from current customers to ensure that the actual buyers reflect the intended audience (if they don't, you've probably unknowingly hit on another market niche!). Of course, if you market to businesses rather than individual consumers, you can glean demographic information about businesses in a certain market segment, as well. This market segment information is a solid foundation on which to build a bigger platform.

DIFFERENTIATION. For a product, service, or brand, the process of differentiation identifies the unique characteristics that distinguish the item from the competition. Special features that translate into distinct benefits to the buyer form the basis for the marketing to a targeted segment.

DIGG. Launched in 2004 and now one of the hottest online sites, Digg shares content from all over the Internet. Readers vote (up or down) the stories and items that are submitted by other Digg users. You'll frequently see items with a link that says "Digg This!" at the bottom, which is encouraging you to vote for the content to boost its recognition on the Digg site. Check it out at digg.com.

DIRECT MAIL. Also known as "junk mail", direct mail takes many forms: postcards, flyers, brochures, catalogs, and those envelopes filled with offers, sales letters, coupons, sweepstakes entries, and sundry other pitches. These hard-copy marketing tools arrive in the mailbox of the addressee courtesy of the U.S. Postal Service. They're the result of a certain amount of market research intended to make the recipient respond to the personal tone of the message. In spite of the naysayers who spout that direct mail is dead, businesses in the United States spent $64 billion on direct mail in 2007, and according to a forecast report by Universal McCann, that number will continue to grow.

DIRECT MARKETING. This marketing approach delivers a promotional message directly to customers rather than through a mass medium. Direct mail and telemarketing are good examples of this. The customer places an order either through the marketer's website or catalog or by actually talking via phone with a customer service representative. The product is then sent from the marketer directly to the customer. Being successful in this simple line of business means that your direct marketing materials are sending the right messages to your customers! If not, they wouldn't be ordering.

DIRECT RESPONSE. Like direct marketing, this type of promotion permits or requests that consumers respond directly to the advertiser by mail, phone, email, etc. These offers may or may not be addressed generically and usually include some sort of special incentive to motivate the response. All those little business reply cards that fall out of your magazines are an example of direct response because they request an action (response) that is sent directly to the advertiser.

DOMAIN. You hear a lot about domains, domain names, URLs, and such. The domain is the Internet address and is usually coded in a series of numbers (e.g., 123.0.0.1). The domain name is the readable version of the domain, such as www.msn.com. The "com" suffix refers to a commercial domain. Others include net (network), org (organization), edu (educational institution), biz (business), gov (government), info (informational resource), mil (military), us (United States), and mobi (mobile phone).

DOT-COM. Referring to the suffix on the majority of web domains, dot-com applies to companies doing business via the Internet. There was a roaring upsurge in dot-com activity from 1995 to 2001, known as the dot-com bubble when businesses hit the Web like piranhas on a feeding frenzy, trying to capture the popular shopping surge happening there. The bubble burst when so many of the dot-coms that had evaded traditional business models exhausted their resources and failed to capture enough revenue to sustain themselves.

DOUBLE OPT-IN. Also known as a confirmed opt-in, the double-opt in uses an added security measure to identify and confirm subscribers. Opting in means accepting an offer to subscribe to an online membership. To confirm that the subscriber is actually the owner of the email address inserted, the site sends an email to you at the address you have registered. You must click on the link in that email to confirm and activate the subscription. The double opt-in has proven to deliver a dramatically higher response rate and has become the preferred method for legitimate emails (i.e., NOT the spammers!).

DYNAMIC PRICING. This pricing model refers to changes in pricing structures based on specific criteria. This variation is used in auction purchasing (e.g., eBay), volume discounts, or at point-of-sale with instant rebates, coupon, buy-get offers, or other incentives.

. . . .

80/20 RULE. It is a commonly accepted theory that 80 percent of a company's business is generated by just 20 percent of the customers. The fiscal power this "rule" yields to those few customers often causes companies to seek a better balance so that they are not at risk of failing if a customer chooses to take its business elsewhere.

E-. With the Internet changing the way we do business in the 21st century, the "e" prefix has come to reflect "electronic". Following is a list of the most common "e-words":

E-blast. An update or bulletin sent via email to a large list of recipients.

E-business. A company doing business on the Internet.

E-commerce. The act of buying and selling on the Internet.

E-mail. Correspondence sent electronically to another user's online address.

E-news. A newsletter sent via email rather than traditional mail.

E-zine. An online magazine.

END-USER. Your product goes from manufacturer, maybe to a value-added reseller, on to a distributor, followed by a retailer, who then sells to the end-user — the person who ultimately does exactly what the name implies: uses it! Depending on your product (or service), you might skip a few steps in the distribution channel. The end-user is the reason you're in business. They are the people or organizations who actually use products and services regardless of whether or not they purchased them. If your crazy aunt buys food for her pet bearded dragon, Cuddles, it is the lizard who is the end-user, (the one who creates the need for the product). Clearly, in marketing considerations, a product must be marketed to *appeal* to the buyer and meet the *needs* of the end-user.

EXPOSURE. Being seen (in a positive light) is the goal of any business owner or marketer. Exposure represents the degree of visibility among a certain segment or in a specific medium or channel.

fF

FACEBOOK. Founded by Harvard University student Mark Zuckerburg as a tool to connect students in an online social network, Facebook has grown to be the network of choice among students, adults, and even businesses, with an estimated 70 million daily active users and 15 billion page views monthly. Facebook provides registered users a place to post their profile (personal data, interests, and fun information) to share with other registered users — for free. As a business forum, Facebook has created something akin to an online mixer for businesses who want to connect with prospects, thought leaders, consultants, and other valuable resources. For his brilliance, Zuckerberg was named by *Forbes Magazine* "the world's youngest self-made billionaire", with an estimated net worth of $1.5 billion by the time he turned 24.

THE FOUR P'S. Just as "reading, writing, and 'rithmetic" are the staples of every elementary school student's studies, The Four P's represent the fundamental marketing principles: Product, Price, Place, Promotion. "Product" refers to the product, which can also be a service, and those features and benefits that distinguish it from the competition's comparable offerings. "Price" reflects the pricing model (low, moderate, high) and considers such factors as elasticity (tolerance for higher pricing) and life-cycle. "Place" refers to distribution, and "Promotion" is the marketing component.

FREQUENCY. Repetition is the key to success in advertising. Frequency is arguably the most important consideration when calculating an advertising schedule. If you can't afford frequency, don't waste your money (see "Shotgunning"). In media buying, "Frequency" refers to the number of ad placements contracted in a given period (e.g., 12 issues per year, 1,000 column inches per month, etc.).

GOOGLE. Is it a proper noun or a verb? The answer is both! Google is the largest search engine on the Internet today, controlling 65.1% of all web searches in the U.S. in 2007 (according to Hitwise, a measurement company). Based on ease of use, billions of indexed web pages in its archives, and free resources (such as Google Analytics), Google has become the search engine of choice and its name has become synonymous with searching the 'Net. With such popularity, Google's advertising programs — AdWords and AdSense — deliver the most common pay-per-click ad buys.

GUERILLA MARKETING. Coined by marketing guru and author Jay Conrad Levinson in his bestselling 1984 book of the same name, this marketing approach relies on simple tools: time, energy and imagination, stealing the thunder from big-budget, waxed and polished marketing tactics. Placing the power and potential for success in the hands of the marketer, this unconventional approach requires you to call on your own personal and professional contacts to help spread the message of your promotion.

The term "guerilla marketing" has become a sort of pop culture lingo. The author says that guerilla tactics are ideally suited for small companies and entrepreneurs because they can be more hands-on with their customers. These principles are the foundation of guerilla marketing:

• Guerilla marketing should be based on human psychology rather than experience, judgment, and guesswork.

• Instead of money, the primary investments of marketing should be time, energy, and imagination.

• The primary statistic to measure your business is the amount of profits, not sales.

• The marketer should concentrate on the number of new relationships made each month.

• Create a standard of excellence with an acute focus instead of trying to offer too many diverse products and services.

• Rather than concentrating on acquiring new customers, aim for more referrals, more transactions with existing customers, and larger transactions

• Forget about the competition and concentrate on *cooperating* with other businesses.

- Guerrilla marketers should always use a combination of marketing methods for every campaign.

- Use current technology as a tool to empower your business.

HIT. In Internet terms, a hit refers to a site being called up by a user. The popularity of a site is measured in the number of hits per day. The more hits you have, the more "traffic" your site is generating and, potentially, the more business you are doing.

HOME PAGE (OR HOMEPAGE). The main page of a website that leads (or should lead) to all other pages on the site. It is important to note that many people have the misconception that visitors enter a site on the home page. In truth, a large number of visitors find a site via an organic search, which can lead them to enter a site from any link, depending on the information they seek. For this reason, it is important to treat every page on the site as a stand-alone, with sufficient data and links to navigate the visitor to other pages, including the home page!

HYPERLINK. With one click on this embedded link masquerading as text, you are automatically transported to a page on the Internet. Hyperlinks can be easily inserted in various technologies, including word processing, emails, and web design. This method is a great way to instantly guide your reader/visitor to a desired place on your website!

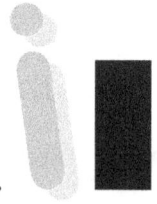

IDEATION. What used to be called "brainstorming" has a 21st century moniker. The process of generating ideas has become a popular buzz word in businesses and organizations that are recognizing the value of encouraging creative thinking. Ideation sessions focus on problem solving, generating ideas for new products or services, developing strategies, and other outside-the-box thinking.

IMAGE ADVERTISING. While some ads promote the specific benefits of a product, service, or event, an image ad presents the brand's image, rather than promoting how or how well it works. Image advertising is primarily used to build an organization's perception within a target market. Image advertising is often used in conjunction with a product-oriented campaign, requiring frequency to reinforce the brand message. Image advertising has no call to action and therefore is nearly impossible to measure, unless you opt for a "before and after" focus group or other market research tool.

Image advertising is often used in situations where an organization needs to educate the targeted audience on some issue, such as dealing with a merger and keeping the focus on what the company offers, not on its politics. These campaigns are also beneficial to rebuilding an image after faltering in the marketplace.

IMPRESSION. The mark, however large or small, that you make on an individual prospect is known in marketing circles as the "impression". It takes numerous impressions to register your message with a prospect. That's why integrated marketing programs are key, because they hit the target from several angles. Sort of like all those planes taking shots at King Kong, but instead of bringing down the monster, you're merely trying to grab their undivided attention. An impression can reflect the number of times a site visitor goes to a particular page, how many vehicles drive by your billboard on a given day or time, and the number of attendees at a trade show or concert who will see your banner hanging in a prominent spot.

You'll hear about "impression counts" and "cost per impression" because marketers know that there is value to increasing the number of impressions you make on an audience. Be aware, however, that some creative accounting can be used to inflate impression counts in order to boost an advertising opportunity's perceived value. You'll see things like "pass along value" built into a magazine's readership figures, which is an educated (and sometimes not-so-educated) guess of how many actual readers look at each copy. The goal is to collect a growing number of visual and/or audio impressions from your specific target in order to reinforce your message through this repetition.

INBOUND LINK. A link that brings a visitor to your site is an inbound link. Relevant links are great boosters to your site, because the search engine crawlers look for this kind of content. The key here is "relevant". Some businesses try to fill up their sites with links but the search engines not only don't fall for it, but they will bump you down in their all-important index for being a link glutton. Your inbound links should be relevant to the content and keywords on your site. Quality needs to trump quantity here.

INCENTIVE. The teaser, bait, or motivator that prompts someone to react in the way you desire, an incentive can take any of countless forms. When considering the incentive in marketing anything, ask *why and how would a customer respond to this?* Consider everything from ease-of-payment to bonus offers to discounts for multiple units. The key is that incentive programs are dictated by your customers' needs and wants. Use the tools at your disposal to key in to those customers and you'll be right on track.

INTELLECTUAL PROPERTY. Often abbreviated to just "IP" these days, intellectual property establishes value for thoughts and ideas. Prior to so much "ideation" in the world today, tangible products were trademarked and great ideas were patented. This vast topic can include patented ideas and plans, copyrighted material, trade secrets, and visions that have not yet reached fruition. There can be financial value for an idea, even in its raw forms, so you need to consider what and how much information you give away, how it will be used, and the actual fiscal value, which can be reflected in the price of your stock.

INTERACTIVE. We have become a culture that is focused on experiences, particularly among Generation Y (born after 1980). Interactive means that the viewer can actually participate in, trigger, or otherwise impact the outcome. For a website, an example of an interactive site is one where you enter information (such as answers to a quiz) and get results. Video game systems like Wii, Xbox, and PlayStation provide an interactive experience for the user. Even reality shows, like American Idol and America's Got Talent, are interactive because audience voting controls the outcome (at least, as far as we know!).

INTERNET. So many people use the proper nouns "Internet" and "World Wide Web" synonymously. So wrong! It is, in fact, a worldwide system of computer networks, linking your computer with all of the others that are accessing this same vast system. Think of the Internet (aka "the 'Net") as the phone company that hooks you up with a phone line so that you can make calls. The Internet connects you with the World Wide Web, which is the keeper of all that great information. So, if you're not on the 'Net, you can't reach the Web (or get email).

INTRANET. This closed network allows access only to authorized users. Such private networks have grown in popularity, particularly in large organizations, institutions, and corporations where information sharing is necessary but requires the security of a firewall.

JAVASCRIPT. This computer language developed by Netscape allows even novice users to create websites with a degree of interactivity.

KEYWORD. Not necessarily a single word, a keyword is a word or phrase that is used during an organic search, to help the user find sites that relate to a desired topic. Keywords are scripted into web pages, indexed by search engines, and also "sold" to the highest bidder for pay-per-click ads.

LANDING PAGE. When you drive traffic to your website, you may or may not want to direct them to the homepage. You might need to send them to a page that features a special offer, something not for the random surfer. The landing page will link this visitor to other pages on your site, and should reflect the brand imaging that exists throughout your site.

LINK. In non-Internet terms, a link is a piece of a chain connecting other pieces. In the online world, a link is a Web URL within a document or web page. Also called a "hot link" or "hyperlink", you can click on this reference to be move directly to that web page.

LINKEDIN. One of countless social networks online, LinkedIn was established for professionals to communicate with one another. This network, which had accumulated 23 million monthly users each month in 2008, represents members from all of the Fortune 500 companies in an online community. Individuals register at no charge, seeking out resources, colleagues, thought leaders, and even job leads. Once you post your profile, you can share information, search for professionals with like experience, knowledge you need, or similar interests. The site is supported financially through advertising.

LINKING STRATEGY. Multiple, relevant links add a powerful ingredient to building a site that gains optimum exposure. An integral part of your search engine optimization (SEO) plan, the linking strategy provides a road map for identifying the links to incorporate, evaluating them for relevancy and quality, communicating with the webmaster for reciprocal linking, and maintaining an ongoing process for doing this. Search engine spiders like relevant links *and* fresh content, so a good linking strategy will boost your ranking. Also, these links allow you to reach more Web users via the links on other sites. The bottom line is, when you effectively increase your web presence, you increase your marketing potential.

LOGO. Your logo is a graphic element for your company's name. It can be as simple as the word itself (IBM, eBay, Disney, FedEx, Yahoo!) or a symbol (the Nike "swoosh, Audi's interlocking rings, or the Macintosh apple) that reflect the core essence of your brand. A logo is often accompanied by a tagline or slogan, to reinforce the brand and its recognition in the mind of the consumer. For example, "You're in good hands with Allstate", "A diamond is forever", and "The milk chocolate that melts in your mouth, not in your hand."

LOYALTY. Loyalty is the result of one positive experience after another with a company that clearly understands the needs (both spoken and unspoken) of its market. When the World Wide Web turned marketing into a global enterprise, loyalty began to circle the drain. With a few clicks, consumers could find what they want, purchasing from a faceless seller. The loyalty to the local bricks-and-mortar retailer began to fade with this boundless "mall." Marketers invest time, energy, and money into understanding how to build loyalty from fickle customers, because maintaining an existing customer costs about one-third of the price to find each new one.

LOYALTY PROGRAM. To promote loyalty from customers who have the option to shop wherever they choose, marketers have flooded the planet with a vast array of loyalty programs. The premise behind such rewards-based programs is to provide incentives for customers to not only continue to buy from your company, but to increase their spending in pursuit of the dangled carrot. Airlines were the early birds with their frequent flyer miles programs. Other loyalty program examples include e-newsletters with coupons and special offers to "subscribers" and private credit cards that offer discounts for using them in their stores.

MARKET PROFILE. As you must know your audience, you must also know your market. A market profile presents a summary of the characteristics of a market, including information on purchasers and competitors, the size of the market, the geographic placement, and a forecast on the buying potential. It can also include basic information on the economic and retail patterns of an area. This information is key to determining your target market and projecting sales.

MARKET RESEARCH. Lest marketing seem like a whole lot of theory, rest assured that beneath it all is a foundation of solid research. Market research refers to the systematic gathering, recording, analyzing, and usage of data relating to the transfer and sale of goods and services from producer to consumer (in other words, "marketing"). This research requires a large investment of time, resources, and finances. Research methods include personal and telephone interviews, snail mail and online surveys, focus groups, and blind shopping (gathering information on a business by acting as a customer and then reporting findings to the market research firm or client).

MARKET SEGMENT. Like attracts like; it's a fundamental law of physics. Take that law and apply it to marketing, and you've got a winning combination. Market segments consist of customers grouped together based on shared characteristics (demographic, psychographic, or a combination of the two). A particular segment can be as large as "U.S. women over the age of 30" or as focused as "Pacific-American women working in the health care field in major metropolitan areas of the U.S." Segmenting in this way divides broad markets into smaller ones (known as "niches"), thus allowing marketers to target their products and services more exactly to the prospective buyers.

MARKET SHARE. Quite simply, the question here is how much is one business selling within a specific market in comparison to competitors? This is expressed as a percentage of the total available market (or market segment) of a product's or service's sales in terms of dollars or units achieved by a brand, line or company. It can be gauged by a company's sales revenue (from that specific market) divided by the total sales revenue (in that market). It can also be expressed in terms of units sold and divided in the same way. Capturing greater market share is the Holy Grail of business. The quest can be just as mysterious based on the influence of the national economic, political, and financial environment.

MARKETING. The basis for all communication between seller and buyer, and the system for influencing a consumer to become a purchaser, through a complex network of tasks, including branding, advertising, public relations, publicity, merchandising, direct mail, sales promotions, and Web-based tools. We are always building or redefining relationships and projecting an image of who we are, what we offer, and why we are essential in our defined market area(s).

Marketing creates the foundation on which leads are generated and/or sales are closed. In general terms, think of marketing as your program that consists of the strategies and tools used to identify, create and maintain positive relationships with customers that result in value for both the customer and you. Done correctly, marketing represents symbiotic relationship where both parties reap the benefits!

MARKETING MIX. Successful marketing does not result from a single effort, such as an ad campaign in one medium. There's an immense interplay of a variety of elements to be considered in the marketing of any product or service. While it has traditionally relied on the 4 Ps (Product, Pricing, Promotion, and Place), the list has a broad array of subgroups for the mix, including packaging, advertising, email, direct mail, public relations, publicity, market research, merchandising, distribution, and marketing budget.

Beyond these tangible things, there's a whole other realm of considerations, most of them beyond the control of the marketer. Economic conditions, legal issues, technological developments, social/cultural changes, political climates, and geographical considerations all play into a product's performance in the marketplace. Ignoring any of these elements could mean leading a marketing campaign down a rocky road or missing a huge opportunity to give it a favorable slant. You must have your eye on much more than just the product or service; you must know the climate in which it will succeed or fail.

MARKETING PLAN. Without a plan for your marketing efforts, you are doomed to fail. Your marketing plan should outline a list of objectives and the specific tasks that will be taken to achieve them. An effective marketing plan will identify the various channels to be used to achieve each objective, a timeline for implementation, an associated budget, and the desired outcomes, such as dollar volume or unit sales, increase in new customers, rise on share-of-wallet, etc. All tasks must be measurable or the plan is really just a wish list.

MASS CUSTOMIZATION. Seemingly a contradiction in terms, mass customization means using the wonders of technology to produce highly personalized products and communication. Through the use of sophisticated software, marketers can direct highly specific communications to customers and prospects, based on the information gleaned from their buying habits. For example, Amazon.com's "People who bought this also bought this" zooms in on a reader's past purchases or views and matches it with other suggestions. Such customized marketing messages have a strong pay-off, with significantly greater response rates.

On the manufacturing side, this same advanced technology allows consumers to "create" their custom product. As an example, Levi Strauss, brand leader in denim jeans for more than a century, faced a significant drop in its highly competitive industry. While the company had retained the loyalty of Baby Boomers, it failed to gain interest from the younger generation. The powers at Levi Strauss identified the problem and launched the Original Spin customization program. Using a computerized kiosk, customers could enter a custom order, choosing the style, cut, color, leg shape, and zipper or button-fly. They entered their hip, waist, and inseam measurements and place the order via the Internet. These customers were willing to pay extra for this personalized fit, which proved that cost-cutting was not the answer; customization was!

Dell's highly successful build-to-order model is another great example of this system at work. Naysayers criticized the company, saying that consumers would never buy a computer over the phone.

The key to successful mass customization, whether from a marketing or manufacturing slant, is building an infrastructure that can support the extra steps necessary to provide this elevated level of service. The added cost, as proven by Levi Strauss, can be passed along to the consumer, if the positioning is done correctly and the market segment appreciates the added value.

MEDIA STRATEGY. When planning your advertising, it is essential to do more than just list the media where you will place your advertising. The media strategy details how you will use the media options to maximize the impact on the desired audience. For example, with Generation Y (those born after 1980) getting their news from the Internet or mobile phones, a company that is targeting this audience would do well to eliminate newspapers from the media mix and to perhaps look more closely at online and mobile ads. To impact business people in a metropolitan area, transit and outdoor (billboard) advertising could present a smart component to the media strategy. Think *who* you're trying to reach and then *where* they can best be reached.

META TAG. The meta tag is an identifier that is hidden within the HTML scripting of your website. These do not affect the function of your site but enable the search engines to find you and match your site to the search criteria of Internet surfers. There are two kinds of meta tags: keywords and description. Keyword meta tags lists words or short phrases that relate to the content of the site. A description meta tag describes the site's content in one or two sentences.

METRICS. All marketing tasks (individual or campaigns) must have a means for measuring the success rate. The statistics gathering process provides a set of metrics for determining all levels of response, including click-through rate, cost per lead, customer acquisition cost, open rate, opt-ins, churn rate, conversion, and other quantitative data that can be used to measure response to a marketing effort.

MOBILE ADVERTISING. Just about anyone capable of making a phone call has a mobile (or cell) phone. With so much usage out there (estimated 2.5 billion subscribers worldwide), and people glued to their phones like a lifeline, the advertising industry has found a new medium for reaching out to consumers. Mobile advertising transmits text messages, graphics, or animated advertisements to cell phones. To grab advertiser revenue, mobile operators have begun offering special incentives to subscribers who agree to receive mobile ads, often in the form of tempting downloads and free text messages. Media analysts estimate that this burgeoning medium will take in $11.4 billion in revenue by the year 2011.

MSN. The acronym for Microsoft Network, MSN is the online service that was launched by Microsoft in 1995, in conjunction with the company's Windows 95. The web-based services include free email (Hotmail), which has approximately 380 million users worldwide, and instant messaging (Messenger), which has accumulated about 225 million users.

MULTI-LEVEL MARKETING. Also known as Network Marketing, this business distribution model allows a parent company to market their products directly to consumers through relationship referrals and direct selling. Sellers are independent and unsalaried, going by myriad titles such as sales associates, franchise owners, independent agents, etc. They represent the parent company and are compensated through commissions based on their sales. These independent distributors grow their own organization both by building their direct customer base and by recruiting their own downline independent distributors, and so on, building a "pyramid" of salespeople.

Actual compensation can be based on several different models. Across the board, though, the bottom line says that the more people you have in your organization — and the more those people are selling — the greater the percentage of total sales volume you receive. MLMs tend to raise eyebrows, having gotten a good deal of bad press in recent years (case in point, Amway). Still and all, they've endured as a primarily grass roots, thriving source of income for millions of people worldwide.

MYSPACE. One of the most popular social networking site on the Web, MySpace ("A place for friends") was launched in 2003 by a group of employees of eUniverse, an Internet marketing company in Los Angeles. Originally targeted at teens who appreciated the creative capabilities for integrating music and video into their personal pages, MySpace has broadened its appeal among older users. What began as a tool for connecting people via the Internet grew to become a valuable marketing tool. The online community of this monstrously successful site has grown to include about 245 million registered users around the world.

NAVIGATION. The structure of a website, or navigation, establishes the movement from page to page, via a network of links. The navigation of a site can be user-friendly or a nightmare. In the case of the latter, visitors get frustrated and beat a hasty retreat. When browsing in the online world, we want speed. Pages that are slow to download, don't exist, or don't allow you to get back to where you came from are problematic. Want to see how you score here? Check your site tracker to see where people are entering, how they move from page to page, and from where they exit. If you're seeing a consistent pattern of short stays and exits from the same place (other than checkout), it's time to rethink your navigation.

NETWORK MARKETING. See "Multi-level Marketing".

NEW MEDIA. When you see the word "new", you have to wonder why the "old" has been replaced. In the case of "new media", the term refers to the emergence of digital communication, as opposed to the "old world" newspapers, magazines, radio, and television. While the existing media still has its place, new media reflects the 21st century surge toward electronic communication, including websites, email, social networking (e.g., Facebook, MySpace), streaming audio and video, online advertising (e.g., pay-per-click), and mobile communications.

NEWS RELEASE. See "Press Release".

NEWSWIRE. Also known as "wire service", this term goes back to the days when news was actually transmitted across telegraph wires. A newswire, like Associated Press (AP), Reuters, and UPI (United Press International) staffs reporters around the world to find stories and report on them via these newswires. News outlets, such as newspapers, magazines, television and radio stations, pay for subscriptions to this service in order to access up-to-the-minute reports as well as obscure stories that can be used as fillers on slow news days. Certain newswires, like PR

Newswire, are commonly used on a fee-paid basis by businesses and public relations professionals that upload their own news stories for distribution to editors and producers. These types of newswires then feed into the larger wires, as well as distributing the news releases to their own media base.

NICHE MARKETING. This targeted marketing strategy zooms in on a highly specific segment, often finding more focused sub-segments within existing customer groups. The niche approach works well for marketers who know how to hone in on smaller segments with unmet needs that can be managedthrough repositioning or consumer education, and not retooling (at least, not significantly) the nature of an existing product or service.

These niches usually develop when potential demand for a product or service is not met by any supply or when cultural, technological or environmental shifts dictate a new and emerging need. Gap, Inc., invested in niche marketing by creating a multi-brand strategy with its three brands: Old Navy, Gap, and Banana Republic. Each retail brand appeals to a different market niche, based primarily on a cost-versus-value perception. In addition, the corporation launched Baby Gap to capture the Gap buyer that was maturing into parenthood. The key to capitalizing on the possibilities in a niche market are making sure that customers are accessible and that the segment is growing quickly and not already owned by another vendor.

To successfully target niche markets, you should do the following:

• Identify segments within the overall, broader market;

• Choose the segment(s) that fits best with your organization's objectives and goals; and

• Develop a marketing strategy that appeals to the selected target market(s).

OFFENSIVE MARKETING. The opposite of "defensive marketing", the offensive approach is a growth strategy that targets the acquisition of new clients and markets, as well as increasing share-of-wallet with existing clients.

ONLINE ADVERTISING. As an advertising medium, the Internet offers tremendous appeal, drawing ad dollars away from the more traditional print media. One tool delivers marketing messages and attracts customers with multi-media elements (print copy, photos, video, audio, affiliate programs, etc). It's fast (allowing instant updates), easy, and the content is unrestrained by geography or time.

The online community affords interactive advertising, which lets consumers peruse a given directory based on product types or brands. The viewer can then visit any given website or interact with the advertiser through email, chat, or by phone. This instantaneous communication means high conversion rates. You can purchase online advertising a number of ways. Here are the four most common:

• CPM (Cost Per Thousand Impressions) means advertisers pay for exposure of their message to a specific audience.

• CPV (Cost Per Visitor, or Cost Per View in the case of pop-ups and unders) charges the advertiser for the delivery of every visitor to the website.

• CPC (Cost Per Click) is also known as Pay Per Click (PPC). Advertisers pay every time a user clicks on the listing ("Sponsored Results") and is redirected to their website. The advertiser pays only when the listing is clicked. This system allows advertising specialists to refine searches using target-rich words (which they bid for) and gain information about their market. CPC differs from CPV in that each click is paid for regardless of whether the user makes it to the target site.

• CPA (Cost Per Action or Cost Per Acquisition) advertising is performance-based and is common in the affiliate marketing sector of the business. The site's publisher assumes all the risk of running the ad, and the advertiser pays only for the number of users who complete a transaction.

OPEN RATE. In a largely virtual business world, having a means to track your effectiveness is invaluable. The email open rate measures how many people open or view your email (as opposed to trashing or ignoring it). Typically measured via an embedded HTML image tag in the outgoing email, your server records an "open" when that image is clicked to open by the recipient.

The method is not totally accurate, however. Some webmail services block images in emails by default, and many people elect to receive "text only"emails. In either instance, when the image does not appear, the message is not counted as opened. Besides, there's no way to tell to what degree people actually read the email even if they open it. But it's a good start!

OPT-IN. This is a term used when someone is given the option to receive bulk email, identical mail sent to masses of people at the same time. This is an easy and efficient way to circulate your marketing message, but obtaining permission to send email is critical to your credibility. Without permission, your message is considered unsolicited bulk email...or spam.

OUTBOUND LINK. A link within a website that sends the user to a page that is not contained within that particular site is referred to as an "outbound link". Relevant links are always helpful because they (1) deliver more information to your user and, thus, improve the perception of your business as user-friendly; and (2) provide a desirable characteristic that search engines prefer. One caveat here: Unless you have a reciprocal arrangement with the other site, your visitor may not be able to return to your site by clicking the "Back" button. This means you've either lost your site's visitor or caused them undue angst by having to find their own way back. In some cases, they may not make the effort, so the outbound link to elsewhere comes at the expense of a possible sale or lead. One way to avoid the problem is to link to those outside sites via a pop-up window.

OVERTURE. See Yahoo! Search Marketing.

PAGE VIEW. The page view is one visit to a page on a website, which determines the traffic level on that page. Also called page impression, this figure is often used by ad reps in their sales pitch to prospective advertisers. A page view (PV) differs from a "hit", which counts the number of times the HTML page and individual components, like images, are accessed. The view refers to the number of times the page itself is loaded.

PAGERANK. This algorithm, trademarked by Google, rates the importance of a web page. Developed by Google founders Larry Page and Sergey Brin, PageRank (PR) determines that page's placement on the search results. The PR is based on a variety of factors, including the number of *relevant* links. PageRank views the links as a "vote" for that particular page, so the more links, the more important the page. However, don't get greedy and use a link farm (a business that is paid to build up your links). That action can (and probably will) backfire because the links are usually not relevant to your site's content and some sites whose links have been cultivated by these farms have been booted off Google.

PARTNERSHIP MARKETING. See "Affiliate Marketing".

PAY-PER-CLICK (PPC). This method of Internet advertising makes the most of technology. Advertisers bid on keywords that surfers would use to find products or services like theirs. These advertisements are called "sponsored links" or "sponsored ads" and are displayed when a user seeks out keywords or web pages with relevant content. The ads appear adjacent to and/or above the search engine results pages or anywhere desired on a content page. The higher the bid, the higher the ad appears on the search results. The advertiser pays only when a user clicks on an ad to visit their website. PPC is used on search engines, advertising networks, and content websites like blogs.

Google AdWords, Yahoo! Search Marketing, and Microsoft adCenter are currently the largest PPC providers. Prices vary and there are two major types of PPC campaigns:

• Sponsored match campaigns display advertisements on search engine results pages.

• Content match campaigns display ads on publisher websites, newsletters and emails.

Either option is a cost-effective way to drive traffic to your message.

PAYPAL. Like the 21st century version of Western Union, PayPal is a paperless means for transferring funds. Established in 2000, this e-commerce business provides an alternative to using checks, money orders, or credit cards for online purchases. The user sets up a PayPal account which is connected to a bank or credit card account. Funds are then deposited or debited to that account, as directed by the user. In this way, the merchant does not have a direct link to the account. Commercial users pay a transaction fee for using PayPal, but the sheer volume of PayPal users almost demands wide acceptance by merchants. In 2002, with more than half of eBay users sending and receiving payments for online auctions via PayPal, eBay acquired the company for $1.5 billion.

PENETRATION. A sales strategy can be horizontal or vertical. The horizontal approach refers to gaining a broader base of clients. With vertical, you dig deeper into the existing customer base, producing more revenue from your loyal customers. The depth to which you dig into this existing base represents your penetration in that segment. Marketers who seek to deepen their penetration look at tactics like: cross-selling, which is selling them additional products they don't usually purchase; and up-selling, or guiding them to more expensive products or a higher volume than they would ordinarily buy, often through creative fulfillment pricing, or payment options.

PERCEPTION. In the marketing world, perception is the way in which a product or service is viewed.

PERMISSION-BASED. The polar opposite of spam is permission-based marketing. In this method, marketers ask permission — naturally — before sending out advertisements to potential customers. It requires that people opt-in before the ad is sent, as opposed to letting them opt-out after the fact. Naturally this approach is a favorite among those with a personal marketing slant. It's much more individualized than market segment or target market methods.

This marketing style is attributed to Seth Godin, a well-known turn-of-the-century marketing guru. He feels that you are essentially purchasing someone's time and they are granting you their attention, more valuable than ever in our current 90-Second Economy.

PERSONALIZATION. Personalization, in marketing terms, refers to tailoring a product or communication to a user based on personal details or characteristics they provide (e.g., through subscriber data, purchases). With a personalized Web page or portal, the changes and content are based on the user's interests and purchasing/viewing history. For emails, personalization means the communication does more than include a personal salutation, but also addresses specific consumer characteristics (including those all-important buying habits).

There are two categories of personalization:

• Rules-based filtering is based on "if this, then that" ("if you bought this, you might like this" and uses a logic program to determine suggestions.

• Collaborative filtering presents shopping suggestions to customers by combining their personal preferences with those of like-minded others ("customers who bought this also bought these items"). This works well for quantifiable products like books, music, videos, craft supplies, and myriad other products that appeal to an interest in a particular genre.

PHISHING. A heinous and illegal practice, phishing is the process of sending emails or making phone calls under the guise of being a legitimate business in order to obtain private information, like usernames, login information, passwords, and credit card details. Spam filters reduce the amount of phishing that gets through but clever phishers know how to circumvent those filters.

PODCAST. A constant stream of new Internet media outlets means that the staples of television and newspaper sources are losing their customer base. On the upside, getting multi-media messages to consumers is easier than ever. One of the most popular methods of doing so is podcasting. Podcasts are audio and video programming that a user can download to a media device — MP3 or video players — for playback at their convenience.

• Audio involves delivering programming via downloadable online audio, such as an iPod or simply iTunes. Many websites and blogs offer free downloadable audio programming.

• Video downloadable for consumer use is relatively new. Many high end sites are constantly experimenting with ways to make the process ad and consumer friendly. Amateur sites like YouTube, though, make it easy for anyone to market their wares.

Smart marketers keep an eagle eye on these emerging technologies. While they're not mainstream today, television news was once scoffed at, too.

POP-UP/POP-UNDER AD. This type of online ad opens a new window in front of the current one, displaying an advertisement or entire web page. A pop-under ad is loaded or sent behind the current window so that the user does not see it until they close one or more active windows. Either way, the ad lays the foundation to get the potential consumer's attention, usually with a one-click call to action to redeem a special offer. They provide essential information with minimal, quickly digestible content. Netflix uses the pop-up/pop-under as an affiliate ad with other websites.

PORTAL. A door, entry, or gateway to the online world, a portal is a point of access, like America Online (AOL), Netscape, and Yahoo! This threshold to the vastness of the World Wide Web organizes and presents information in an easy, one-page, at-a-glance way. Setting up your browser to a portal like Yahoo! gives you a page that categorizes general information with links to entertainment, world news, sports, shopping, stock reports, real estate, and travel. You also link to your personal webmail, weather reports, and instant messages.

POSITIONING. The process of positioning a product or service is used to establish its differentiation from competitive products and then communicating that position to the targeted market segment. A positioning statement summarizes, in just a couple of sentences, the key benefits and the value proposition in an effort to influence the buyer. For an in-depth look at this topic, refer to the timeless bestseller by advertising giants, Al Ries and Jack Trout, *Positioning: A Battle for Your Mind.*

PRESS RELEASE. A news/media/press release communicates newsworthy items to the media with the objective of getting press coverage. Preferably condensed to one or two pages, the release is written in journalistic style as a news report, not an advertising piece. Blatant sales messages will get ignored by editors and producers, in favor of those releases that respect their commitment to delivering items of interest to their readers, viewers, and listeners. Use a press release to announce new hires, promotions, new products or services, events, and human interest stories. There is a specific press release format preferred by journalists, so be sure to consult the *AP Stylebook.*

PRICING. The selling cost you associate with your product or service makes the most direct impact on your bottom line, although it is tightly connected with the other 3 "Ps" of the marketing mix (Product, Place, Promotion). Pricing strategy must take into consideration more than the actual cost of producing and delivering the product. Competition, elasticity, product lifestyle, and various other factors should influence price. Pricing can reflect a variety of strategies, including these common options:

- **Competition:** influenced by the pricing of competitive products or services.

- **Cost-plus:** adds a fixed percentage to the actual cost of producing and delivering the product/service.

- **Dynamic:** a flexible pricing model that presents different pricing depending on factors such as distribution channel, geographic location, market segment, and elasticity.

- **Market-oriented:** based on the demand and tolerance of the target market.

- **Penetration:** setting the price low enough to influence buyers and grab market share, a common strategy for pricing a new brand with no existing customer base.

- **Premium:** setting the price high, in spite of actual cost, in order to establish a perception of heightened quality to increase appeal to a market that desires such distinction.

PRODUCT BUNDLING. This promotional strategy packages two or more packages together at a "bargain" price. Bundling usually involves packaging a new or under-selling product with one that has established demand. Bundling is intended to put a product in the hands of consumers so that it can be sampled — a proven effective means of driving sales!

PRODUCT PLACEMENT. This advertising opportunity creates an almost subliminal impression. Rather than a blatant advertisement or celebrity endorsement, a product placement features a product within a television show or movie. The subtle association of celebrities using particular brands is believed to influence buyers. What began as game show placements with prizes has become a powerful marketing tool where advertisers pay to see their products in the hands of celebrities. From the appliances used on Extreme Makeover Home Edition to the omni-present Coke cups in front of the judges on American Idol to the hot cars driven in the latest action movies, the act of seeing products in context has created an intriguing bridge between the advertiser and the filmmaker and television producer. While placements have dropped off in the past year, this advertising venue continues to generate big dollars.

PSYCHOGRAPHICS. For the serious marketer (with a serious need for deeper information than just demographics AND serious time and money to invest for the information), there is psychographics. This term describes consumers on the basis of psychological characteristics such as values, lifestyle, personality, attitudes, and opinions. While demographics (which are quantitative) identify a prospect's compatibility with a certain product or service, psychographics (which are qualitative) measure their likeliness to purchase, based on these motivators. When you can gain both demographic and psychographic information about a market segment, you can more effectively target their needs and anticipate buying behavior.

PUBLIC RELATIONS. The PR component focuses on building positive relations with the public, using the media's reporting to communicate newsworthy stories. "No news is good news" is not the case with a PR professional, whose goal is to get editorial coverage that keeps the client's name in the press, in a favorable way. Creating the perfect, supportive blend of organizations, products/services, and media outlets is the goal of any good PR firm or department and its campaigns. With all of the media and technology now available to us, the role of modern PR includes:

• Building awareness and a favorable image for a company or client within stories and articles found in relevant media outlets (which are triggered by the PR person's press releases or story pitches to the reporter/editor).

• Closely monitoring numerous media channels for public comment about a company and its products.

• Managing crises that threaten the company or product image.

- Building goodwill among an organization's target market through community, philanthropic and special programs and events.

All of these tools come together so that public relations efforts support marketing by building product/service and company images. In a world that espouses "image is everything," a good PR platform is essential to the longevity of any company that wants not just survival, but growth!

PUBLICITY. It was once explained that if the circus is coming to town and you create a sign that announces the event, that's advertising. Next, you hang the sign from an elephant and parade it around town and it happens to tromp through the mayor's flower garden. Then you get publicity. When you get the mayor to laugh about the incident, that's public relations. When all that comes together, people have more awareness of the event. So they buy tickets. That's sales!

Publicity is the act of bringing attention to your business in a way that grabs the attention of the media. Unlike press releases that communicate a story, publicity is most often tied to an event. Actors, singers, authors, and other public figures will appear more frequently in the news and on talk shows when they are pitching a new show, movie, book, CD, or other item they want the public to purchase. Publicity can be as simple as distributing posters and flyers or as complicated as a well-timed stunt. Having a chorus line of men dancing in their boxers in Times Square, for example, certainly brought TV cameras to film the spectacle, giving great coverage to the uncoverage!

PURE PLAY. This term refers to a business that is focused solely on one product or service category rather than diversifying the mix. Coca Cola, which has limited its product line to beverages, is a pure play company, while its major competitor, Pepsi, has branched out to food products (Frito-Lay and Quaker brands). A pure play company could also be one that limits its marketing and distribution channel, such as an Internet (dot-com) business that exists only in the virtual world and has no bricks-and-mortar physical storefront.

PUSH-PULL STRATEGY. If you want your marketing campaign to be really successful, you have to hit take aim at your targets from more than one direction. A push-pull strategy is implemented to push your distribution channel to both actively promote your product and purchase more of it. The pull comes into play by then reaching out and grabbing your end-user by the collar and directing them to your resellers. Driving buyers to those resellers motivates them to support your product, because you're supporting them. And, for those who aren't supporting your business, well, they can either buy the product to satisfy demand or risk losing them to someone else who can deliver those goods.

QUALITATIVE RESEARCH. Market research should be an integral driver of your marketing strategy and tactics. The qualitative side of your research provides data on the psychological aspect: perceptions and attitudes. Unlike quantitative research, which crunches hard numbers, the qualitative studies boost the marketer's knowledge of the consumer mindset. This data is most often gathered through personal interviews and focus groups, where open-ended questions prompt conversation, which unearths some valuable insights. When it comes to information-gathering, you can go after quantity or quality, but one side is not exclusive of the other.

QUANTITATIVE RESEARCH. This research component is a statistician's dream! The research is designed to provide numbers, numbers, and more num-bers. Quantity, percentages, frequencies — these are all key evaluators for measuring consumer habits. This type of research is most often con-ducted via surveys (personal, phone, email, and snail-mail) with closed-ended questions. The goal is to gather data, not promote conversation. For more in-depth consumer perceptions, build in qualitative research.

R

RATE CARD. Used by media representatives for selling ad space, the rate card outlines costs, mechanical specifications, discounts, and other production information. The rate card is one part of the overall media kit, which usually contains a demographic profile, readership study, editorial calendar, and competitive comparison. Rate cards are often the starting point for negotiation with the ad rep. You can often get frequency discounts without committing to the full frequency or negotiate value-added bonuses to sweeten the deal.

REACH. How far do your marketing arms extend? Reach refers to the estimated number of people in the audience you are targeting.

READERSHIP. In the language of print media, you have "readership" and "circulation". They are not synonymous. Circulation is the number of printed copies produced per issue. Readership takes this number and creates an estimate of how many people actually purchase and/or read the issue. This is accomplished by "pass-along value", a figure that represents an estimation of the number of readers per copy. If a magazine has a circulation of 500,000 and a pass-along value of 2.2, then they will present the readership as 1,100,000. You can qualify these figures when there is an audit of the circulation. This audit provides you with actual distribution figures, both by state and acquisition (subscription, newsstand, unpaid). Readership figures do have value but should be carefully evaluated, since they can be subjective.

RECIPROCAL LINK. When creating outbound links to other sites, you need to establish a reciprocal link from their site in order for the user to be able to return to your site by simply hitting the "Back" button. The reciprocal link means that both webmasters agree to build a hyperlink in their sites to allow easy interchange from one site to the other — and back again. You can bypass the situation by having the outbound link open up in a pop-up window that can be clicked close rather than actually shifting the user to the other site.

RELATIONSHIP MARKETING. This marketing approach focuses on the development of long-term customer retention versus the individual transaction. Building a foundation on customer satisfaction, relationship marketing recognizes the fiscal value of loyalty; it costs three times as much to acquire a new customer as it does to maintain an existing one. Personalization, value-added services (like Best Buy's Geek Squad and Apple's Genius Bar), and loyalty programs are common ingredients in a relationship marketing program. CRM software (see "Customer Relationship Management") is an integral component to the success of relationship marketing because a powerful customer database delivers the detailed information, just like the engine of a high-performance car. CRM includes such psychographic details as customer preferences, likes/dislikes, interests, activities, and buying habits.

RESPONSE RATE. A term used in direct marketing (direct mail, email, telemarketing) that refers to percentage of people who responded to the ad or offer from the total number of people contacted. The higher the response rate, naturally, the more effective your ad. According to the Direct Marketing Association, which rates the responses for 19 different media channels (e.g., coupon, direct mail, catalog, magazine ad), telemarketing still generates the highest response rate, with statement stuffers, magazine blow-ins, and newspaper display ads ranking the lowest. Business-to-business (B2B) campaigns generate a slightly higher response rate than business-to- consumer (B2C). Direct mail, like post cards, brochures, and catalogs, deliver an average response rate of 2-3%.

RICH MEDIA. This term refers to the wealth of interactive media living within the Internet, including streaming video and mouse-overs (images that change when the mouse's cursor moves over it).

RUN OF NETWORK. When buying advertising time on a cable television network, you can specify particular programs in which to air your commercial (for an added fee) or choose "run of network", which means the commercial will air at any given time during a particular span (often 12 or more hours). A major advantage of cable network advertising is that the programming for each network is targeted at highly specific demographics (e.g., children for Nickelodeon, teens for MTV, men for ESPN, women for Lifetime). Conversely, the prime networks (ABC, CBS, NBC, Fox) are not market-specific as the audience can significantly change by the hour. Run-of-network offers a cost savings but you still need to be aware that your commercial could be buried in a weak time slot.

RUN OF PRESS. An ad purchased for print media can be placed within a particular section (e.g., Sports, Entertainment, Finance) or spin the wheel and take the "Run of Press" option. ROP can place your ad anywhere. You can request the front section, outside right hand page, or above the fold, but without paying a premium, such placement will not be guaranteed.

RUN OF STATION. A radio or television commercial can be aired at any time during a wide span of time, as designated by the network. These commercials are most frequently used as fillers during early morning and late evening hours. Don't expect prime time for these bargain rates!

SATURATION. In chemistry, you learn that when you mix more Kool-Aid than the amount of water in your glass can hold, the result is sediment sitting at the bottom of your glass. This is saturation. A market has maximum tolerance for the amount of product it can absorb (i.e., purchase). Once you've saturated your market, the excess inventory sits on the shelves, like sediment in the bottom of your glass. When you hit that saturation point in the product's lifecycle, don't just shelve it and lose the return on your considerable investment. There are still options for growth. You can make improvements, upgrades, and updates to your product and revisit your market. Look at the parade of new car models every year, the replacements of cell phones for something with sweeter features, and the sale of personal computers to customers who need to keep up with ever-changing technology.

SEARCH ENGINE. If you've ever gone to the Internet in search of anything, you were guided by a search engine. Gone are the days when your fingers do the walking or you do your homework by flipping through an enormous encyclopedia of outdated information. Now, you go to the keyboard. Thanks to the Internet, computer programs search through massive amounts of text or other data to get us what we need. A search engine's job is to find all possible websites that use the words specified in the search. There are many search engines, but Google, Yahoo! and MSN are the most popular. So universal is Google in fact, that "google" has become a verb meaning "to search for". You simply type in the word or phrase for what you are looking for (your "keywords") and the search engine's program sifts through billions of pages to find the best matches.

SEARCH ENGINE MARKETING. The amount of business you can do via the Internet can be limited by the heavy hand of the search engines. Gaining greater visibility here is key to driving more traffic to your site. Search engine marketing is a component of the online marketing strategy that focuses on building that visibility. Tools such as Pay-Per-Click (PPC) ads, search engine optimization (SEO), paid inclusion and feed management, and Web analytics. Search engine marketing is as complex as the engines themselves; it is no place for novices so if you want to explore this area, talk to a pro.

SEARCH ENGINE OPTIMIZATION. To the businessperson trying to build an online presence, the search engines (e.g., Yahoo!, MSN, Google) can seem like the dark lords of this vast empire, and their crawlers/spiders are the flying monkeys. In the early years of the Web, clever hackers figured out how to out-smart the search engines in order to gain a higher place on the results page. But the lords prevailed. Now, if you want to appease them to get that improved visibility, you need to optimize your site, which is simply playing by their rules. SEO is the process of managing the content of your site to align with the ways in which the search engines' algorithms search and index pages. The use of appropriate keywords, refreshed content, and relevant, ample links is a great start. SEO is an ongoing process. If you want to keep up with the other citizens in the kingdom, you must manage your site, feed the flying monkeys, and make nice with the dark lords.

SEARCH ENGINE RESULT PAGE. Any time you search the Web for information, the search engine you're using posts a list of matches to your keywords — a list that can go on for more pages than you could possibly view. You'll often see this abbreviated as "SERP"

SEGMENTATION. Breaking down a market into subgroups with common threads is a target marketing strategy that allows for customized products and promotions that address the more focused needs of this segment. This technique allows you to appeal to multiple smaller markets with strategies tailored to the unique demands of each; one large market is divided into smaller, more distinguishable ones. Increasingly, consumer product firms are offering multiple products under the umbrella of one large category. Everyone needs shoes, for instance, but not everyone needs baby shoes or work boots. Some people need basketball shoes while others need walking shoes, and so on.

SERVER. A Web server acts like a host to you, the client. This computer is dedicated to responding to your requests to access HTML pages and files. The server is a designated computer and usually runs a specific server application, such as Web, file, mail, or proxy server. Any computer can act as a server, but it usually has a faster CPU and more memory to act as a more effective storage unit.

SHOPPING CART. Online shopping is made easier with the use of a virtual shopping cart. The customer clicks this icon to access the page on a site to accumulate products for purchase. Behind the visual aspect of the shopping cart that the customer sees, there lies a complex software program that makes the shopping experience as easy and secure as possible for the purchaser. Too often, the process of shopping and checkout becomes so time-consuming for the consumer that the cart is abandoned and the purchase is never completed.

SHOTGUNNING. Advertising success depends on repetition and frequency. Shotgunning refers to the practice of running ads in various media, with little or no frequency. Without getting deep enough penetration in any particular medium, the advertiser doesn't get results, only a large media bill. Buying media intelligently is like gardening. If you have a large field and a limited amount of manure to fertilize it, you can spread the fertilizer thin over the whole field and get reduced results, or you can focus on a patch of the garden and tend it with ample amounts of manure to cultivate a large harvest. Reap the most from your investment and put the shotgun away.

SKYPE. With Skype, you can turn your computer into a telephone. Once you download the Skype software, you can make calls around the world, even if they aren't using Skype (although calls from one Skype user to another are free). The program allows for video conferencing, conference calling, instant messaging, and file transfer. Launched in 2003 by a team of software wizards in Estonia, the company was purchased for $2.6 billion by auction giant eBay in 2005.

SOCIAL NETWORK. A social network is an online community of people who share common interests, ideas, professions, concerns, religion/faith, political views, ethnicity, and likes/dislikes, to name just a few connecting threads. Social network sites have exploded in popularity, fueled by the extraordinary success of leaders like MySpace, Facebook, and Flickr. A step above the chat rooms that prevailed in the infancy of the Internet, social networks connect millions of people through a multi-tiered approach where one user can connect with the friends of friends (or colleagues, professional connections, or other valuable resources). First introduced to Web surfers by Friendster in 2002, there are now countless social networks existing around the world and used by millions. With such numbers, marketers have jumped on the social networking bandwagon, using their pages to communicate with prospects in an atmosphere similar to a cocktail party, with casual chatter and no hard selling.

SPAM. What was once just an odd luncheon meat product of unknown origin has come to mean unsolicited bulk email. Spammers are those who use non-permission-based email lists (i.e., names of people who have not opted-in to receive messages) to communicate with large numbers of individuals. At best, spam with a legitimate message can acquire new leads, depending on the relevance of the list, but most frequently, it's as annoying as getting piles of junk mail in your mailbox (although email saves trees and has no outside costs for printing or postage). At worst, spam infiltrates the recipient's computer with a virus or scams unknowing people out of money or credit information. You can avoid spamming by legitimately grabbing subscribers who have expressed interest in receiving communication from you.

SPIN. A common term among public relations professionals, "spin" is the positioning of a story, giving it a twist to make it more interesting, less damaging, or to otherwise craft the message so that it gains positive results.

SPIDER. This creepy crawler is a software program used by search engines to review the content on websites and index them for later reference. When a Web user surfs for information on a particular topic, the spiders (also known as "crawlers") scramble through the index and find the best matches to the keywords typed in for the search. Search engine spiders feed on fresh content and relevant links, so if you feed them appropriately, your pages will get better play on Web searches.

STREAMING MEDIA. "Streaming" refers to the delivery method of audio and/or video, animation, synchronized graphics, or illustrated audio to a computer via the Internet. The media is sent in a "flowing" stream and the user can then view it as it is arriving, without waiting to download the entire file. This is a huge advantage for adding media to a website without the lengthy delay required for downloading large files.

SWOT ANALYSIS. When framing a marketing strategy, it is beneficial to take an inventory of the components in your "toolkit". This can be accomplished by conducting a SWOT Analysis: Strengths, Weaknesses,

Opportunities, and Threats. The exercise, when done objectively, provides valuable perspective on the internal (strengths and weaknesses) and external (opportunities and threats) factors the organization faces. "Strengths" identifies the positive traits of the company and its products or services. "Weaknesses" are the organizational flaws that hinder pursuit of objectives. These weaknesses are valuable because repairing them usually presents an opportunity for growth. "Opportunities" reflect unrealized potential for gain, such as flawed competition, economic shifts that promote spending, legislation that creates need and demand for upgrades or retrofits, or niches that are not yet penetrated. "Threats" represent external situations or conditions that will challenge the system. Planning a strategy to meet these threats is similar to dealing with weaknesses in that the ability to rise to the challenge may create new opportunities.

TACTIC. A tactic is a specific action to be taken in order to meet an objective that is outlined in a strategy.

TAGLINE. Also called a "slogan", a tagline is a short phrase that reflects a product's or service's brand identity, usually communicating a benefit. For example, Coca Cola's timeless tagline "It's the real thing" is intended to reinforce the soda's uniqueness and its distinction from "copycats". Here are a few other classics: "The Few. The Proud. The Marines." "Don't leave home without it." (American Express); "It keeps going and going and going." (Energizer Batteries); "We bring good things to light." (General Electric); "Good to the last drop." (Maxwell House Coffee); "You're in good hands with Allstate."; "When it rains, it pours." (Morton Salt); "All the news that's fit to print." (The New York Times).

TARGET MARKET. Know your audience. Then get them in your sights. The target market is the segment that represents the demographics and/or psychographics that best match your product or service. This group of customers are qualified to make purchases of the products or services that a marketer is able to offer. Qualified customers are defined as those who:

• seek a solution to a need (spoken or unspoken)

• are eligible to make the purchase

• are financially capable of making the purchase (e.g., credit qualified)

• have the decision-making authority

Whether it's breakfast cereal or designer shoes, identifying not only who wants to buy but also what qualifies them to buy is essential. The better you know your target, the sharper your aim!

TECHNORATI. Technorati (a combination of "technology" and "literati") grew from the powerful growth of blogging on the Internet. This blog search engine indexes nearly 113 million blogs. Technorati also tracks social media, podcasts, and vlogs (video blogs). Although the site has come under fire for its somewhat boastful claims, it is still a highly rated search engine

TEXT MESSAGE. The next generation of paging, text messaging (or "texting") sends a message to from one mobile phone or PDA (personal digital assistant, like a BlackBerry, iPhone, Treo, or Palm) to another, using SMS (Short Message Service). Like any other successful technology, texting has been embraced by the marketing community. Mobile marketing uses texting to reach cell phone users and to get them to respond to offers by means of texting. With the omnipresence of cell phones, mobile marketing and texting will play a significant role in the future of business.

TREND ANALYSIS. It's been said that if you don't learn from the past, you're doomed to repeat it. By remaining aware of current and upcoming trends

— in sales, marketing, products, services, delivery — and having a solid grounding in history, the visionary business person or entrepreneur possesses a wealth of growth opportunities, whether that information prompts a chance to expand your product/service line to meet greater needs or you discover a glitch in your system that, when fixed, can enhance your sales forecast. But what do you do with what you know? First evaluate the trends you've identified, noting them as short-, mid-, or long-term trends. Identify the market segment(s) for these trends. Can you determine the cause of sales trends? Look at this information with an objective viewpoint, as hard as that may be, and look at the symptoms that are both subtle and blatant. From this point, give yourself a prescription for making the changes you need to improve the outlook.

TYPEPAD. Blogging is quite possibly the fastest growing strategy for building business online. All it takes is a little help from a blogging service, and TypePad is the most popular among the fee-based services. You can certainly go for the free services, like Blogger ad WordPress, but Type-Pad delivers more for the monthly fee.

UNIQUE SELLING (SALES) PROPOSITION. Before you can effectively promote your business, product, and/or service to the end user, you need to clearly define your distinction from the competition. Know what sets you apart so you can communicate that benefit — your unique selling proposition — to your market. Your USP is a key part of positioning (see "Positioning"). Remember that low price is not a good USP because this point can be easily taken away simply by having a competitor drop prices. Instead, look for the uniqueness (or perceived uniqueness) within your core business. Federal Express has become synonymous with guaranteed overnight delivery and has focused intently on delivering on that promise; so, while competitors can provide the same service, FedEx maintains the peak position in its industry by reinforcing its position in every element of its marketing and advertising. To identify your USP, identify your core business, profile the market you serve, and then determine how you will use your strengths to meet the needs of that market. In a short statement, communicate exactly what your end user can expect from you.

UNIQUE VISITOR. While many odd characters come to mind here, in marketing terms, a unique visitor is a statistic describing a unit of traffic to a website, counting each one only once in the time frame of the report. In other words, a person returning to the site from the same Internet account is not counted more than once. The statistic measures a site's true audience size, just as "reach" (as discussed earlier) does for broadcast media. The number of total visitors divided by unique visitors results in the derived "Average Sessions Per Unique Visitor" in the specified time.

This information is captured in two ways:

• by requiring all visitors to log-in to the site, thereby capturing the identity of each visitor on each visit

• by placing a cookie on each visitor's computer, writing the cookie ID to a database, and checking for the cookie on each visitor's computer each time they visit.

Either way, this is a useful tool for keeping up on your site's relevance and visibility.

UNSUBSCRIBE. Spamming (unwanted email) prompted legislation to protect people from getting "junk" email. The option to "unsubscribe" gives you the freedom to be removed from a mailing list. Often, this option is exercised by clicking on a link, but other emailers will request that you send an email with the unsubscribe request.

USER-GENERATED CONTENT. A few years ago, marketers didn't just send out advertising messages to the end users of the world. They started *receiving* them. User-generated content (UGC, because we are a society obsessed with acronyms) is the label that describes the two-way communication that erases the boundary between seller and buyer. McDonald's customers who were so jazzed by the fast food chain's fast food that they created their own, homemade commercials, saw themselves in prime time as marketers recognized the positive impact of such a powerful testimonial. UGC can come in many forms, from a simple blog posting or photo to a digital video, commercial, web page, or wiki (see "Wiki"). Just like television's reality shows have turned the average American into a television star, UGC gives the end user a supporting role in the viral marketing of their favorite products.

VALUE PROPOSITION. Take your USP (see "Unique Selling Proposition") and clearly articulate the benefit to your end user in one or two sentences. Make a statement that answers the question: What's in it for the customer?

VERTICAL MEDIA. Look at the broad reach of media topics that stretch across the horizon. General categories like men's interest, women's fashion, travel, and finance are considered horizontal media because they span a wide range. Vertical media, on the other hand, penetrate deeply within a topic, to address the interests of a highly targeted market. Industry trade journals and websites, for example, represent vertical media. When you are considering niche marketing, vertical media will likely have a place in your plans.

VIDEO NEWS RELEASE. Have you ever watched the evening news and seen a human interest story or learned about a new product or service that is changing the way you live? Most of these "news items" have been prompted by a video news release. Similar to a written release, a video news release is used to convey information in a newsworthy manner. Using video and a journalistic style, the release is a short treatment, created to entice the media to cover the "story", either airing the release as is, bits of it wrapped into another story, or coming to your place of business to film an original story! Just remember that this release is a news story and not an advertisement. To be successful, look at your story from the perspective of a television producer who is bombarded with pitches. Then communicate a newsworthy message in an objective, journalistic manner.

VIRAL MARKETING. If spreading a cold or computer virus can be so exponentially easy, why not use the metaphor for spreading good news, too? This popular type of marketing refers to using pre-existing social networks to increase brand awareness and product sales. The message can be spread by word-of-mouth or Internet networking and is based on voluntary and authentic enthusiasm, infusing it with a certain credibility.

The average person tells three people about a product or service they like and eleven people about one they don't like. Human nature just begs to deliver a message and one marketer coined the phrase for this phenomenon. Harvard Business School professor Jeffrey Rayport wrote "The Virus of Marketing" in December 1996 for *Fast Company* magazine. Numerous researchers have run with the term, making it fodder for countless articles and blogs.

The key to using viral marketing is to identify people and/or organizations with high Social Networking Potential (SNP) that can create messages with momentum. A great mass-scale example of this is the 2008 film *Cloverfield*. It was first publicized with a teaser trailer that did not advertise the film's title, only its release date: "01·18·08." Elements of the viral marketing campaign included MySpace pages created for fictional characters and websites created for fictional companies alluded to in the film. Brilliant…and very successful.

VISITOR. Someone once said, the best guests are ones you don't have to make a meal for! In today's fast paced, virtual environment, the best guests are probably visitors to your website, which means anyone who clicks into your site either directly or through links, sponsored or otherwise. Visitors are the touchstone of the success of the Internet component of your business.

WEB DIRECTORY. Also called a *link directory*, a web directory resides on the World Wide Web where actual human beings, not software, categorize websites. Different from a search engine, it does not work from key words. The categorization is based on the whole website type. Directories can be broad or niche in scope, taking into account languages and regions, in addition to other categories. Most allow site owners to submit their site for inclusion and work with editors to review them for suitability. Yahoo! Directory and Open Directory Project (also known as DMOZ, short for Directory Mozilla) are popular ones.

WEB 2.0. First, there was the World Wide Web, and it changed the way we live, work, shop, and communicate. But that wasn't quite enough. Once we had the Web, we wanted to turn it into a forum that would open the door and let us in where we can be an active part of the online world and its communities. So Web 2.0 was born. Social networking, digital videos, blogging, and wikis are a few examples of the second generation of life on the Web. And, while the facet that distinguishes the first iteration of the Web from Web 2.0 are the social connections, from a business perspective, this type of networking is a proven means for mixing business with pleasure.

WEBSITE (AKA WEB SITE, WEB SITE, WEBSITE). A website, however you spell it, is the collection of connected pages that you develop and upload to the World Wide Web under one URL or domain address. Your site can include outbound links, but only those pages developed and maintained under your domain constitute your website.

WI-FI. You see the term on signs for hotels, restaurants, cozy little corner cafes, airports, and even the waiting room in a car dealership. But do you know what it actually means? A take-off of the term hi-fi (for high fidelity radio), Wi-Fi is actually a trademarked proper noun meaning "wireless local area network (WLAN)". This technology omits the need to "hard wire" your laptop to a modem in order to access Internet service. It lets you use your smart phone or PDA (assuming you have Wi-Fi connectivity on your device) to grab your emails or get online to surf the Web. A "hotspot" is a location where a Wi-Fi connection is available (free or for a fee).

WIKI. A wiki (or "Wiki" depending on your preference for proper nouns), is the result of the passion that Web users have for being interactive. From the Hawaiian word "wikiwiki" (meaning fast), a wiki is a server software program that allows a visitor to openly edit the content of a website that is not his/her own. The outsider can step in and add, delete, or change text, graphics, hyperlinks, and even games. The degree to which a site can be "wikified" is determined by the program. Not all wikis are created equal.

WIKIPEDIA. The days of relying on outdated encyclopedia for answers are gone. WIkipedia is a free, online encyclopedia that was launched in 2001 by entrepreneur Jimmy Wales and philosophy professor Larry Sanger. The name was derived from "wiki" which refers to open editing by users, and "pedia", short for encyclopedia. Completely user-generated, the content is prepared and submitted for free, allowing individuals to wax eloquently on any topics in which they are highly knowledgeable. Currently, there are approximately 1.3 million such articles on Wikipedia in English, but the site is also growing in other languages (translated in about 100 other languages and in 11 language editions with their own content). Although every entry is reviewed by Wikipedia, errors still occur. Citations for reference sources are strongly encouraged, and alerts will pop up on entries that have not been verified. So, while Wikipedia appears as a tempting shortcut for quick information, you might want to double-check the information before quoting it elsewhere.

WORD-OF-MOUTH (WOM) ADVERTISING. A heartfelt testimonial is perhaps the best, most credible form of advertising, as it carries the credibility of an outside source. When that testimonial is shared via word-of-mouth, the credibility factor soars! Referrals have proven to be the best source of new business, so companies are relying more heavily on the viral impact of WOM. If you can get people talking about your business, you've cleared a major hurdle because people will *feel* the message in what they're being told. You can spend thousands of dollars on an ad campaign with an emotional punch… but you can also deliver a product that people get excited about and let them spread the word for you!

WORLD WIDE WEB (AKA WWW OR THE WEB). The proper nouns "Internet" and "World Wide Web" are not synonymous, although there seems to be considerable confusion as to the distinction. The Web represents the collection of sites that are available by connecting to the Internet. So, the Internet is the actual connection; the Web is the unending source of information. Without an Internet connection, your door to the vast Web library is locked. The documents that are available on the Web are scripted in HTML (HyperText Markup Language) to make them user-friendly. The Web was conceived in 1980 by Englishman Tim Berners-Lee, a contractor for the European Organization for Nuclear Research (CERN) in Switzerland. Eventually, with the support of Belgian computer scientist Robert Cailliau, the initial concept was presented in 1990 to the European Conference on HyperText Technology. A year later, the Web became available to anyone connected to the information highway.

yY

· ·

YAHOO! Unless you've been stranded on a deserted island that has not been invaded by a reality show, you know that Yahoo! is one of the top (if not number one) search engines that exists on the planet. What began as a pet project by two Stanford University graduate students David Filo and Jerry Yang (who wanted to find a way to catalog the personal favorites on the Internet) has become a worldwide leader in Internet communications, commerce, and media. Yahoo! (an acronym for "Yet Another Hierarchical Officious Oracle") serves about 345 million people each month.

YAHOO! SEARCH MARKETING. This brand is Yahoo's pay-per-click (PPC) Internet advertising service. The PPC medium allows advertisers to buy "Sponsored Results" that will show up on the search results page when the keyword(s) for the search match those of the advertiser, thus allowing a business that doesn't have a high page ranking to get visibility at or near the top results. Placement for these ads is based on the bid price of the advertiser: the higher the bid for a keyword, the higher the place-ment. With Yahoo! Search Marketing and any PPC service, the advertiser only pays the bid price when a visitor actually clicks on the ad's link and goes to the landing page of the advertiser.

What began as Goto.com in 1998 became Overture in 2001 and was highly profitable when Yahoo! (Overture's best customer) acquired the company in 2003 for $1.7 billion. Yahoo! eventually renamed the com-pany to align with its other brands (e.g., Yahoo! Finance, Yahoo! Travel, Yahoo! HotJobs).

VOCABULARY LISTS

Build your knowledge of MarketingSpeak in the areas of your specific interest. Maybe you need a crash course on Web jargon or advertising media. Use the lists below to look up the words you should know.

ADVERTISING

AdWords
AdSense
Advertiser
Advertising
Call To Action
Campaign
Circulation
Co-op Advertising
Demographics
Exposure
Frequency
Image Advertising
Impression
Keyword
Logo
Media Strategy
Mobile Advertising
Online Advertising
Pay-Per-Click
Perception
Pop-u/Pop-under Ad
Psychographics
Rate Card
Readership
Run of Network
Run of Press
Run of Station
Shotgunning
Tagline
Vertical Media
Word-of-Mouth Advertising
Yahoo! Search Marketing

CHANNEL STRATEGY

Affiliate
Affiliate Marketing
Cannibalization
Channel Distribution
Channel Marketing
Channel Promotion
Direct Mail
Incentive
Loyalty
Loyalty Program
Multi-level Marketing
Partnership Marketing
Pure Play
Push-Pull Strategy
Reach

CUSTOMER RELATIONSHIP MANAGEMENT

Brand Loyalty
Client
Customer
Customer Relationship Management
End-user
Incentive
Loyalty
Loyalty Program
Permission-based
Relationship Marketing

DIRECT MARKETING

Campaign
Channel Marketing
Channel Promotion
Database Marketing
Direct Mail
Direct Marketing
Direct Response
End-user
Logo
Personalization
Response Rate

EMAIL MARKETING

Auto-responder
Campaign
CAN-SPAM
Channel Marketing
Channel Promotion

Click-through
Click-through Rate
Database Marketing
Double Opt-in
E-blast
E-business
E-mail
E-news
E-zine
Hyperlink
Landing Page
Link
Logo
Open Rate
Opt-in
Permission-based
Personalization
Phishing
Response Rate
Spam
Text Message
Unsubscribe

MARKET SEGMENTATION

Client
Customer
End-user
Market Profile
Market Segment
Niche Marketing
Penetration
Psychographics
Reach
Segmentation
Target Market

MARKETING METRICS

Break-even Analysis
Churn Rate
Click-through Rate
Cost Per Conversion
Metrics
Open Rate
Qualitative Research
Quantitative Research
Response Rate
Trend Analysis

MARKETING MIX

Advertising
Channel
Channel Marketing
Channel Promotion
Direct Mail
Direct Marketing
Direct Response
E-commerce
E-mail
Four Ps
Marketing Mix
News Release
Online Advertising
Press Release
Pricing
Product Bundling
Product Placement
Public Relations
Publicity

MARKETING STRATEGY

Action Plan
Affiliate
Affiliate Marketing
Article Directory
Article Marketing
Brand/Brand Identity
Business Plan
Buzz
Buzz Marketing
Campaign
Channel Distribution
Channel Marketing
Client
Customer
Database Marketing
Defensive Marketing
Differentiation
Direct Mail
Direct Marketing
Dynamic Pricing
80/20 Rule
E-commerce
End-user
Guerilla Marketing
Ideation
Incentive
Intellectual Property
Logo
Loyalty
Loyalty Program
Market Research
Market Share
Marketing Plan

Mass Customization
News Release
Newswire
Niche Marketing
Offensive Marketing
Partnership Marketing
Penetration
Personalization
Podcast
Positioning
Press Release
Pricing
Product Placement
Product Bundling
Public Relations
Publicity
Pure Play
Push-Pull Strategy
Qualitative Research
Quantitative Research
Relationship Marketing
Saturation
Segmentation
SWOT Analysis
Tactic
Target Market
Unique Selling Proposition
Value Proposition
Viral Marketing
Word-of-Mouth Advertising

ONLINE MARKETING

AdWords
AdSense
Banner Ad
Blog
Blogger
Blogosphere
Bookmark
Browser
Buzz
Buzz Marketing
Campaign
Database Marketing
Domain
Dot-com
E-business
E-commerce
Exposure
Google
Hit
Internet
Intranet
Landing Page
Link
MSN
New Media
Newswire
Online Advertising
Opt-in
Overture
Page View
PageRank
Pay-Per-Click
PayPal

Permission-based
Personalization
Podcast
Pop-up/Pop-under Ad
Viral Marketing
Web 2.0
Website
World Wide Web

SEARCH ENGINE OPTIMIZATION

Algorithm
Blog
Blogger
Blogosphere
Bot
Cookie
Domain
Google
Hyperlink
Inbound Link
Internet
Intranet
Javascript
Keyword
Link
Meta Tag
Outbound Link
Page View
PageRank
Search Engine

Search Engine Marketing
Search Engine Optimization
Server
Spam
Spider

VIRAL MARKETING

Blog
Blogger
Blogosphere
Digg
E-mail
Facebook
Internet
Intranet
LinkedIn
MySpace
New Media
Social Network
Technorati
Text Message
TypePad
User-generated Content
Viral Marketing
Web 2.0
Wiki
Wikipedia
Word-of-Mouth Advertising
World Wide Web
Yahoo!

WEBSITE DEVELOPMENT

Algorithm
Analytics
Blog
Blogger
Blogosphere
Bookmark
Browser
Cookie
Digg
Domain
Dot-com
End-user
Google
Hit
Home Page
Inbound Link
Internet
Intranet
Javascript
Keyword
Landing Page
Link
Linking Strategy
Meta Tag

MSN
Navigation
Outbound Link
Page View
PageRank
Portal
Reciprocal Link
Rich Media
Search Engine
Server
Shopping Cart
Skype
Spider
Streaming Media
Technorati
Unsubscribe
User-generated Content
Web Directory
Web 2.0
Website
Wi-Fi
Wiki
World Wide Web
Yahoo!

ACRONYMS

Our culture has become obsessed with labels, in an attempt to categorize issues, products, concerns, and basically anything that needs to be identified and filed within a group. And when those labels become too much of a mouthful, we quickly resort to the acronym. So, as an FYI, here is a list of commonly used acronyms in the marketing world.

AOL. America OnLine

B2B. Business to business

B2C. Business to consumer

CPC. Cost per click

CPA. Cost per action

CPM. Cost per thousand

CPS. Cost per sale

CRM. Customer relationship management

CTR. Click-through rate

FAQ. Frequent asked questions

HTML. Hypertext Mark-up Language

IM. Instant message or messaging

IMC. Integrated marketing communication

IP. Internet protocol; also intellectual property

ISP. Internet service provider

IT. Information technology

KISS. Keep It Simple, Stupid

MSN. Microsoft Network

PFP. Pay for play

POS. Point of sale

PPC. Pay per click

PPL. Pay per lead

PR. PageRank, public relations

PV. Page view

ROI. Return on investment

RON. Run of network

ROP. Run of paper/press

ROS. Run of station

RSS. Really simple syndication

SEM. Search engine marketing

SEO. Search engine optimization

SERP. Search engine result page

SMS. Short message service

TCP/IP. Transmission Control Protocol/Internet Protocol

TOMA. Top-of-the-mind awareness

UGC. User-generated content

URL. Universal resource locator, uniform resource locator

USP. Unique selling proposition

WIIFM. What's in it for me?

WOM. Word of mouth

WWW. World Wide Web

ABOUT THE AUTHOR

A dedicated marketing professional, Michelle Kabele has been helping technology companies develop award-winning channel partner programs and marketing strategies for over 10 years. Her innovative channel marketing concepts have been adopted and implemented by many leading technology companies, including Zebra Technologies, 3Com Corporation, and U.S. Robotics.

Moreover, Michelle has worked extensively with VARs throughout North America and thoroughly understands the realities and practicalities they face in planning and executing effective promotional, marketing, and sales campaigns.

Michelle has an MBA from the J.L. Kellogg Graduate School of Management (Evanston, IL) and an undergraduate degree from Northwestern University (Evanston, IL). For more great ways to build your business, check out all of Michelle Kabele's books:

Great Marketing Is Free!

All the Web's A Stage

50 Smart, Easy and Effective Ideas to Boost Your Business Today

Visit www.ideastormpress.com for up-to-the-minute news, advice, ideas, and just cool stuff.

www.ingramcontent.com/pod-product-compliance
Lightning Source LLC
Chambersburg PA
CBHW060647210326
41520CB00010B/1780